S0-BTT-476

UPDATE:
AIDS

by Mark McCauslin

Crestwood House
Parsippany, New Jersey

Cartoon drawings by Jim Kirschman

PHOTO CREDITS

Cover: Ellen Neipris
Ellen Neipris: 6, 11, 26, 33
AP Wide World Photos: 8
Brian Vaughan: 20

Copyright © 1995 by Silver Burdett Press

Published by Crestwood House, an imprint of Silver Burdett Press.
A Simon & Schuster Company
299 Jefferson Road, Parsippany, NJ 07054

First edition
Printed in the United States of America

10 9 8 7 6 5 4 3 2 1

Library of Congress Cataloging-in-Publication Data
McCauslin, Mark.
     AIDS / by Mark McCauslin — 1st ed.
          p.   cm. — (Update)
     Includes index.
     ISBN 0-89686-812-5
      1. AIDS (Disease)—Juvenile literature. [1. AIDS (Disease).]
 I. Title. II. Series: Update.
     RC607.A26M378   2995
     616.97'92—dc20   93-27798
     Summary: Discusses the AIDS epidemic with an emphasis on AIDS in the United States and how the disease affects society. Includes a listing of organizations that provide information about AIDS.

Contents

Understanding AIDS

THE WORLD'S #1 HEALTH CONCERN

AIDS—the very word stirs emotion in all of us. We feel everything from fear and denial to anger and guilt to sympathy and confusion.

It's hard to believe that the word AIDS has been in use only since 1982. Since then, AIDS has become a leading topic in the news, in schools, and in the arts.

In a brief period of time, AIDS has turned our world upside down. It has forced us to confront our fears, challenge our beliefs, and question our choices.

So much is still unknown to us about the disease. That's what makes it so frightening. But many facts have been discovered since the early 1980s. Understanding these facts is the best way to end the AIDS crisis.

Did You Know...?

- **Percentage of AIDS Cases Worldwide**
  Africa: 69 percent   **United States: 16 percent**
  North and South America (excluding the U.S.): 9 percent
  Europe: 6 percent   **Other: 1 percent**
  Source: World Health Organization. Numbers have been rounded.

- **More than 200,000 Americans have died from AIDS. That number is greater than the combined total of American deaths in the Korean, Vietnam, and Persian Gulf wars.**
  Source: *When Someone You Know Has AIDS*, by Leonard J. Martell

- **It is estimated that nearly 2 million people have AIDS worldwide.**
  Another 14 million people are thought to be infected with HIV.   Source: World Health Organization

- **In the United States, the average age of death from AIDS is 35.**   Source: *Newsweek*, January 18, 1993

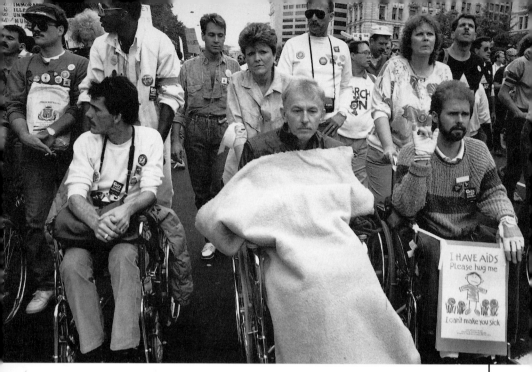

People with **AIDS** and their supporters march in a demonstration in Washington, D.C.

Where Did AIDS Come From?

AIDS has been in the news only in recent years. But researchers now agree that the virus that causes AIDS has been around since the 1950s.

A **virus** is a germ that exists in humans, animals, and plants. Viruses cause a variety of illnesses. Warts and the flu, for example, are each caused by a different virus. The one that is believed to cause AIDS is called **HIV**—short for human immunodeficiency virus.

No one is sure where HIV came from. But researchers have discovered an almost identical virus in certain African monkeys. These researchers believe that somehow this virus was spread to humans. Perhaps it happened when scientists were doing experiments with monkeys and humans in Africa in the 1950s.

Some researchers believe that HIV has existed for thousands of years. The earliest known example in humans is from several blood samples taken in Africa in 1959. A handful of mysterious deaths there in the 1960s are now thought to have been from AIDS. Ten years later, the disease had become widespread in much of Africa.

Researchers in the 1970s were unaware of what was causing these deaths. Meanwhile, visitors to Africa were sometimes exposed to the virus. When they returned to their homes, they spread the virus to others.

Haiti is an island nation south of the United States. Many Haitians worked in Africa in the 1970s. It is believed that they brought the virus home with them unknowingly. By the end of the decade, the disease had become a major problem in Haiti.

In 1981, doctors in the United States were treating patients for an unusual type of pneumonia and a rare type of skin cancer. Many had already died. All of these patients were homosexual men.

A **homosexual** is a person who is sexually attracted to members of the same sex. Another word for this is **gay**. A person who is attracted to members of the opposite sex is called **heterosexual** or **straight**.

Originally, doctors thought that only gay men could get this disease. They named the disease **GRID**, or gay-related immune deficiency. At first, neither the government nor the

Magic Johnson's Story

The world was stunned when Magic Johnson announced his retirement from basketball in 1991.

Magic had everything going for him. He was the Los Angeles Lakers' star basketball player. He was making millions of dollars endorsing products on television. He had been recently married and was going to be a father.

But he also was infected with HIV.

"I got HIV because I had unprotected sex," Magic says in his book <u>What You Can Do to Avoid AIDS</u>. "I got HIV because I thought HIV could never happen to me."

Although Magic has retired from playing professional basketball, he hasn't given up on life. He now devotes his time to educating people about HIV and AIDS.

"Until we accept that anybody can get HIV, the epidemic is going to continue to grow," he believes. "Education and the courage to change risky behaviors are our best weapons against HIV."

"Magic" with HIV positive children at the UCLA Medical Center

media showed much interest in the disease. Because of a lack of funds and support, research was slow and limited. Most people seemed to dismiss the illness as a "gay disease." But soon straight men and women were becoming sick with the disease.

In 1982 the disease was officially renamed AIDS, or acquired immunodeficiency syndrome. At that time, no one knew what was causing AIDS.

A year later a French researcher discovered a virus found only in the blood of AIDS patients. It is widely believed that this virus is the one that causes AIDS. The virus was later called HIV.

Within the next ten years, AIDS became the number one health concern around the world. There is still much to learn about the nature of HIV and AIDS. But doctors have come a long way in such a short period of time.

What Is HIV?

The virus that causes AIDS is so small it cannot be seen by the naked eye. When this tiny organism is first introduced into a person's body, it attacks a type of blood cell called **T cells**.

T cells are part of our **immune system**, which protects the body from disease. When we are exposed to viruses or bacteria (another kind of germ that can cause illness), our immune system tries to destroy them so that we won't get sick. And if we do get sick, the immune system fights to make us well again.

HIV takes over a T cell when the virus enters the body.

The cell then produces more HIV. These will enter other T cells and take them over as well.

This pattern continues until almost all the T cells are destroyed. At this point, the immune system becomes too weak to fight off simple germs or infections. And it is too weak to help a sick person get better.

Someone with a weakened immune system has a serious health problem. For example, a woman with healthy T cells might be exposed to the virus that causes the common cold. Her immune system could kill the virus to prevent her from becoming sick. Even if she did get sick, her healthy immune system would fight the virus so she would recover in a day or two.

But imagine that a woman with fewer T cells is exposed to the same cold virus. Her weak immune system wouldn't recognize the threat of infection. She would probably become sick. And she would not get better in a few days. In fact, the cold could turn into something more serious, like pneumonia. In her case, a simple cold could become a life-threatening illness.

When someone with HIV begins to have severe reactions to common ailments, we know that his or her immune system is failing. This individual has gone from being infected with HIV to having AIDS.

What Is AIDS?

When HIV enters a person's bloodstream, he or she will develop symptoms similar to the flu. These symptoms will appear two to six weeks after infection. They include fever, sore throat, skin rashes, coughing, and a variety of other ailments.

After that, no more symptoms will appear for a while. People who have the virus are called **HIV-positive**. Those who do not are **HIV-negative**. HIV-positive people can feel healthy for months or even years before developing symptoms of AIDS. During this time, however, they can transmit the virus to others, even though they don't seem sick themselves.

About 80 percent of people with HIV will develop AIDS

An **AIDS** patient is examined by a doctor.

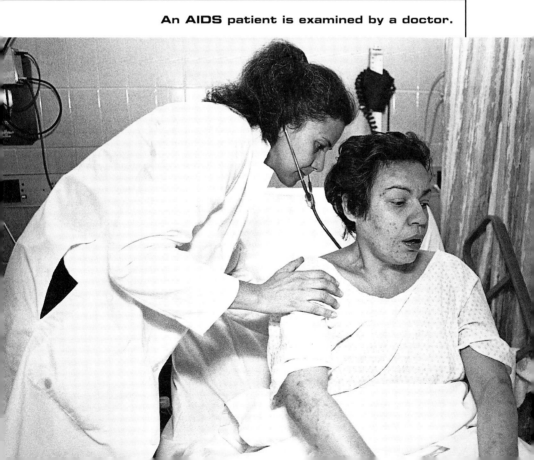

within ten years of the initial infection. The early symptoms of AIDS are similar to those for other diseases. Only a doctor can tell you if you have AIDS or not.

The early signs include these:

- *Low energy level for several months*
- *Sudden, unexplained weight loss*
- *Swollen glands in your neck, underarms, or groin*
- *Fevers that linger for months*
- *Diarrhea that lasts for weeks*
- *Excessive sweating while you sleep*
- *Skin rashes*
- *Allergic reactions to common medications or insect bites*
- *Flu symptoms that last for a month or longer*

Once a person has full-blown AIDS, he or she can develop dozens of other ailments. The immune system is so weak that it cannot fight off most kinds of infection. Some of the most common symptoms include the following:

- *A dry cough or shortness of breath*
- *Purple or red areas on the skin, usually on the arms or legs (probably caused by a rare skin cancer called* **Kaposi's sarcoma)**
- *A thick, whitish coating inside the mouth (from a yeast infection called* **thrush***)*
- *Clusters of small, painful red blisters*
- *Easy bruising*
- *Unexplained bleeding*

- *Change of mood and loss of memory (these could be symptoms of AIDS **dementia**, a brain disorder)*

As an AIDS patient's immune system gets weaker, it is unable to fight off even the most simple infection. Eventually one of these infections might cause the patient to die.

It is unknown if all people with AIDS will die from it. Some people have had the disease for ten years or longer. Unfortunately, they are in the minority. Most people die within two or three years of developing AIDS.

Because AIDS is a life-threatening disease, we all must take precautions to protect ourselves. The key to preventing AIDS is understanding it.

HIV INFECTION: THE FACTS

Did You Know...?

• In recent years, deaths from cancer were down by 2 percent.
Deaths from heart disease were down by 8 percent.
Deaths from AIDS were up by 175 percent.

Source: *When Someone You Know Has AIDS*, by Leonard J. Martell

• Reported U.S. AIDS Cases by Type of Transmission
Homosexual sex: 57 percent
IV drug use: 23 percent
Homosexual sex and drug use combined: 6 percent
Heterosexual sex: 6 percent
Blood transfusions: 2 percent
Hemophilia treatments: 1 percent
Other: 5 percent

Source: Federal Centers for Disease Control and Prevention

• About 75 percent of people with AIDS throughout the world are heterosexual.
About 90 percent of new infections involve hetero-sexuals.

Source: *What You Can Do to Avoid Getting AIDS*, by Earvin "Magic" Johnson

• In the United States, a teenager gets a sexually transmitted disease every 13 seconds.

Source: *Understanding Sexual Identity*, by Janice E. Rench

14

Doctors have known about HIV only since the early 1980s. They are learning new things about the nature of the virus every day.

Because knowledge of the virus is new to us, many myths and rumors have been spread by people who don't know the facts. These people are afraid of the disease and confused about all the new medical information.

It's important to separate the facts from the fiction. Knowing how you can and cannot get HIV can help you avoid getting AIDS.

How You Can Get HIV

HIV infects a person's blood cells. Blood cells are found in a person's body fluids. The four body fluids that are known to transmit HIV are blood, a man's semen, a woman's vaginal fluids, and breast milk. Saliva, tears, and sweat are also body fluids, but researchers don't think HIV can be transmitted through them.

In order for infection to be passed from one person to

WHAT'S YOUR BEST PROTECTION?

GUN

KNIFE

CONDOM

another, the infected body fluids of a person with HIV must enter the bloodstream of a noninfected person. The two most common ways for this to happen are by having sex and by sharing needles while taking drugs.

There are three kinds of sex acts that are high-risk and can easily lead to infection—vaginal sex, oral sex, and anal sex.

Vaginal sex occurs when a man's penis enters a woman's vagina. Oral sex occurs when a person uses his or her mouth to stimulate a partner's sex organs or anus. Anal sex occurs when a man inserts his penis in the rectum of a woman or of another man.

The vagina, the rectum, the mouth, the area around the eyes, and the hole in the penis are lined with **mucous membranes**. These membranes are spongy, moist layers of cells. Mucous membranes are more sensitive than the skin on the outside of our bodies. Their lining can rub off or tear easily, especially during sex.

When HIV-infected body fluids come into contact with mucous membranes, it's easy for the virus to be absorbed by the layers of cells. And if there is a small tear in the membrane lining, it is even easier.

People who take drugs intravenously—by injecting the drugs into their veins—are also at risk if they share **IV needles**. When a person takes drugs this way, a small amount of blood is left in the needle. If another person uses this needle, that blood passes directly into his or her bloodstream.

There are other ways that HIV can be spread, too. A pregnant

Rita Lytle's Story

Rita Lytle is a 21-year-old college senior who will be graduating soon with honors. She is also the founder of an AIDS-awareness group on her campus.

"I've always been proud of my school achievements," she says. "I've worked hard, studied a lot, and the results have been worth it."

But there was one day when Rita wasn't so smart. "I can still recall it as if it was yesterday. It was three years ago, during my freshman year. I had been to a party and had too much to drink. Then the guy I was hanging out with passed me a joint.

"Well, one thing led to another and soon we were back at my room, making out. We started having sex, but we weren't careful. I was so wasted, I didn't even think about safer sex!

"I couldn't believe it the next day. I mean, I know a lot about AIDS. I'm not stupid. Well, not usually, anyway. I guess drugs and alcohol can make a person stupid."

Although she had unsafe sex only once, Rita is HIV-positive. Now she shares her story with others to help them avoid AIDS. "But all the knowledge in the world about HIV and AIDS can't protect you from infection," she says. "You have to put that knowledge to work."

woman with the virus can pass it on to her unborn child. Or a mother can give it to her child while breast-feeding.

A number of people have become infected after they were in an accident or had an operation. They lost so much blood that doctors gave them blood **transfusions**. Unfortunately, these patients received blood that had been donated by people who had HIV.

Similarly, some patients have become infected when they received body organ **transplants**, such as a new heart or kidney, from someone who had HIV. And some people who have **hemophilia**, a rare disease that makes them bleed easily, have become infected from the blood products used to treat their disorder.

Since 1985, however, doctors have been able to test blood and blood products for the virus. The risk of getting the virus from donated blood or organs is now very low.

Having your ears pierced or getting a tattoo with the same needle that was used on a HIV-infected person is another possible way to get the virus.

Some people are afraid that their doctor or dentist could infect them, through either physical contact or the use of contaminated tools or needles. In fact, two women in Florida got AIDS from their dentist, who had the disease. Experts are unable to say how this occurred. Some people have even suggested that it wasn't an accident—that the dentist deliberately infected the patients to bring the AIDS issue to national attention. In any case, this kind of transmission is nearly impossible if your doctor or dentist uses gloves, a mask, and sterilized tools while examining or treating you.

How You Can't Get HIV
The virus that causes AIDS dies fairly quickly once it is outside the body. It's not like cold or flu viruses, which can travel in the air. You can't catch HIV from a toilet seat or a coffee cup or a cigarette or a towel. You can't get infected from food or drink, even if it was prepared and served by someone with HIV.

You can't get the virus from a mosquito or from a pet.

Since the virus lives in a person's bloodstream, you can't catch it from casual contact with an HIV-infected person. This means you can play sports or dance with anyone without taking a risk. You can hug or shake hands with anyone, even if he or she has AIDS.

A casual, dry kiss is also safe. Doctors don't think open-mouth kissing is a high-risk activity, but it may not be completely safe. If both partners have a cut or bleeding gums, it might be possible to pass on the virus.

Other sexual activity is, of course, unsafe. Many people are choosing another option—**abstinence**. Because they are deciding not to have sex, they aren't at risk. They are still able to date and dance and hug and kiss.

People who are sexually active, however, must be very careful. No method of sex is completely risk free. But there are steps you can take that will give you more protection. Practicing these measures is called having safer sex.

To help protect yourself from the AIDS virus, a condom should always be used when having sex.

Safer Sex

Safer sex is any kind of sexual contact that does not allow one person's semen, vaginal fluids, or blood to come into contact with his or her partner's vagina, penis, anus, mouth, or eyes.

The key to safer sex is the **condom**, a rubber sheath that fits over a man's penis. A condom prevents the penis and semen from coming in direct contact with the partner's sexual organs and body fluids. The best kind of condom to use is made of latex rubber. If you are having vaginal or anal sex, make sure the condom is coated with **nonoxynol-9**, a sperm-killing lubricant that also helps kill HIV.

Use a latex condom every time you have sex, even if you are having oral sex. Never reuse a condom. If you use a lubricant, make sure it says "water-based" on the label. Lubricants that are oil-based, such as hand lotion, Vaseline, or vegetable oil, can cause the condom to break.

Your mouth should never come in direct contact with your partner's sex organs or anus. If you are performing oral sex on a man, he should wear a condom. If your partner is a woman, she should cover her sex organs with a **dental dam**—a large square of latex rubber. A cut-open condom or a piece of strong plastic wrap (such as Saran Wrap) can also be used to cover a woman's vagina.

If you have a small cut on your finger or hand, do not touch your partner's body fluids or sex organs.

Avoid alcohol and drugs before you have sex. They can make you careless and allow you to have unsafe sex. They also weaken your immune system, making it easier to become infected.

You should also limit the number of sex partners you have. The more partners you have, the greater your chance of coming into contact with HIV. Remember, a person can look perfectly healthy but still have HIV.

For safer sex to be as effective as possible, you must practice it every time you have sex. Although there is still a small amount of risk involved, safer sex is the only option if you want to be sexually active and remain healthy.

Testing for HIV

Researchers have developed a test to see whether a person has HIV. There are two reasons why someone might want to get tested, especially if he or she has had unsafe sex or has shared needles.

First, the sooner HIV infection is diagnosed, the sooner it can be dealt with. There are medical treatments and life-style changes that can prolong an HIV-positive person's life, but they are most effective before AIDS symptoms develop.

Second, a person can be HIV-positive and not have any AIDS symptoms. Knowledge of HIV infection will help prevent the carrier from passing it on to someone else.

The test itself is a simple one. A health-care worker takes a small sample of blood from the patient's arm with a needle. The sample is sent to a lab to be tested. The patient gets the results in one or two weeks.

Once HIV enters the bloodstream, the immune system

tries to fight it off with **antibodies**. These are small particles in the bloodstream that attach themselves to the virus. When a patient takes the HIV test, a doctor analyzes the blood sample for the presence of these antibodies. If they are present, the patient is assumed to be HIV-positive.

After a person is infected, it takes anywhere from three to six months for enough antibodies to develop so they can be detected by the test. Therefore, a person who becomes infected today will not test positive for several months. But during this time, he or she can still spread the virus to others.

If a person tests positive for HIV, another test is taken to confirm the results. If the second test is positive too, a third test is taken to be sure the results are correct.

If a person's first results are negative, another test should be taken in three or six months, especially if he or she might have been exposed to HIV recently.

If you are interested in being tested, talk to someone you can trust. A parent, teacher, or doctor can help you decide if the test is necessary. Learning the results can be frightening, and you'll need emotional support if you test positive.

There are many clinics that do anonymous testing. They don't ask for your name, and they don't give out the results to anyone but you. Many of these clinics also do the test for free. To find one in your area, call one of the hot lines listed in the back of this book.

PEOPLE AT RISK

YOU CAN'T CATCH H.I.V. FROM:

CUPS

TOILET SEATS

HANDSHAKES

INSECTS

PETS

HUGS

TOWELS

Anyone can get AIDS. The virus that causes the disease can infect anyone, whether black or white, gay or straight, rich or poor, young or old. Who you are or where you live has nothing to do with infection. It's what you do that puts you at risk.

Many people think that AIDS is a "gay disease" or a "junkie disease." They think they're not at risk if they don't have homosexual sex or shoot up drugs.

This kind of thinking is dangerous—and deadly. Many straight people who don't take drugs are now infected with

Did You Know...?

- In the United States, African Americans and Latinos make up 21 percent of the population. But they make up 46 percent of all U.S. AIDS cases.
  Source: *Good Health for African Americans*, by Barbara Dixon

- An HIV-infected woman who is pregnant has a 25 to 40 percent chance of passing the virus to her unborn child.
  Source: *Good Health for African Americans*, by Barbara Dixon

- Approximately 10,000 children in the United States have been infected with HIV by their mothers. There are 1,500 to 2,000 new cases each year.
  Source: *The New York Times*, March 21, 1993

- By the year 2000, there will be about 72,000 children in the United States whose mothers have died of AIDS.
  Source: *The New York Times*, March 21, 1993

- Since 1990, the number of AIDS cases among young women has nearly doubled.
  Source: *When Someone You Know Has AIDS*, by Leonard J. Martell

- In a survey of gay male teenagers, more than half of the young men admitted to having unsafe sex.
  Source: *Time* magazine, August 3, 1992

- In U.S. prisons, 28 percent of all inmates die of AIDS.
  Source: ABC News

AIDS affects everyone. Here a man holds a poster at the 1992 democratic convention asking what candidates planned to do about the AIDS epidemic.

HIV. In fact, the virus is spreading fastest through heterosexual sex.

Some groups of people are especially at risk for infection. Some of these groups have been associated with the disease since the beginning. Others are developing AIDS at an alarming rate.

Gay Men   The 1960s and 1970s was a time of change in the United States. Americans were tired of the war in Vietnam and of social inequalities. Minority groups demanded equal rights in business and social situations. African Americans, women, and homosexuals were among the groups that led the protests.

Before this time, most homosexuals had kept quiet about their sexual orientation. Many gay men and women had felt isolated. But once they became more open about their sexuality, they realized they were not alone. These men and women were now experiencing a freedom they had never had before.

For gay men, this new freedom enabled them to experiment with their sexuality, which led to **promiscuity**. Being promiscuous is having many sex partners. With this wave of promiscuity, sexually transmitted diseases such as syphilis and gonorrhea spread rapidly among many gay men. There wasn't cause for too much alarm, however, because these diseases are curable.

But this was before AIDS existed in the United States. In

the 1980s, when AIDS was first recognized, gay men were the only people known to have the disease. Doctors didn't know the cause, and research on the subject was slow and limited. In the meantime, gay men were unaware that they or their sex partners could be carrying a deadly virus.

Since many gay men had many sex partners, the disease spread quickly throughout much of the gay community. As a result, about two out of every three Americans with AIDS today are gay men. These men didn't get the virus because they had homosexual sex. They got HIV because they had unsafe sex.

HIV is often spread from one drug user to another when they share intravenous needles.

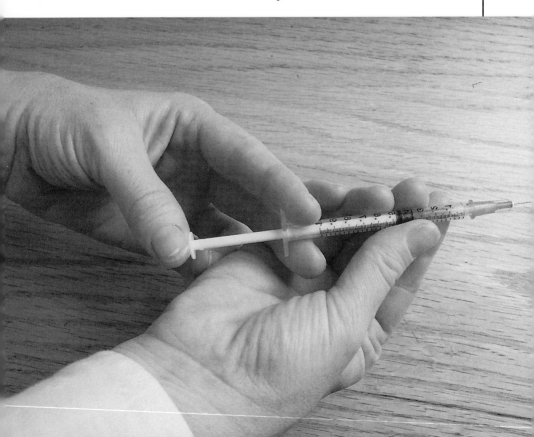

AIDS has mobilized members of the gay community. They have set up groups to raise money for research and to help people with AIDS. And they have spent time educating people about safer sex and the dangers of promiscuity.

With this increased awareness, the rate of new HIV infection has decreased slightly among gay men. The decrease is proof that education about HIV and AIDS is the most effective tool we have in preventing the spread of the disease.

IV Drug Users

When some social barriers were broken down in the 1960s and 1970s, many changes occurred. Minorities were treated more fairly. Women had more opportunities in the workplace. A clean environment and peace between nations became important issues.

Encouraged by a new sense of personal freedom, some people experimented in ways that were once socially unacceptable. Unfortunately, not all of the activities that people tried were good ones. Just as sexual promiscuity became widespread, so did the use of drugs.

IV drugs are taken with a needle, and IV drug users often share their needles with other users. This is how HIV has spread so quickly among these men and women. In the United States, they are the second-largest group infected with HIV.

Using IV drugs is one of the quickest ways to get HIV. When sharing needles, IV drug users often inject a tiny drop of another user's blood directly into their own bloodstream.

And because the users are often addicted to the drug, their immune system is already severely weakened. They are more likely to become infected with HIV.

Actually, researchers are convinced that the use of any recreational drug puts a person at risk for HIV. A recreational drug, such as marijuana or cocaine, is one that is taken for the "high," or the excitement. These drugs weaken the immune system, so a person using them is more likely to become infected when having unsafe sex.

The IV drug user isn't the only one at risk. A person who stopped injecting ten years ago could still be carrying HIV. That means that a sex partner could be exposed if the couple does not have safer sex. And then other sex partners of these two people could be exposed. This kind of chain reaction is probably how AIDS has spread into the heterosexual community.

Obviously, the best way for an IV drug user to avoid HIV is to seek treatment and stop using drugs. If that is not possible yet, the drug user should avoid sharing needles, cotton, and spoons.

Receivers of Blood Products
HIV has also infected some people who have received blood transfusions, an organ transplant, or blood products to treat hemophilia. These people received blood products donated by someone who had HIV.

Since 1985, all donated blood and organs are tested for the

Elizabeth Glaser's Story

Elizabeth Glaser was a woman whose life was greatly altered by HIV. Her husband was Paul Michael Glaser, an actor who starred in the TV series "Starsky and Hutch." After the couple married, they had two children.

Everything was going great for Elizabeth. Then her young daughter developed AIDS.

At first the parents were shocked. They couldn't imagine how their child could have become sick. But once everyone in her family was tested, Elizabeth learned that she was also HIV-positive. She had become infected with the virus years earlier when she received contaminated blood in a hospital.

Apparently, she had passed on the virus to her daughter during breast-feeding. The tests also revealed that her son was HIV-positive.

The Glasers' daughter died in 1989. A few years later Elizabeth helped found the Pediatric AIDS Foundation. This group offers aid and support for children with AIDS and for their families.

Elizabeth died in December 1994. Although her life was cut short, she will be remembered for her accomplishments. In the book <u>What You Can Do to Avoid AIDS</u>, she said, "I'm proud that I've been able to do something positive with a situation that seemed so full of nothing but negitives."

virus. Unfortunately, the test is not a guarantee against contaminated blood. Some blood donations can contain HIV but still test negative. And there have been several instances in which contaminated blood has been used because of faulty hospital testing.

But the risk of contracting AIDS this way is very small. Still, some people who are planning surgery donate their own blood before the operation, in case they need it.

Women and Children   In the 1980s, most of the people known to have AIDS were gay men, so women were thought to be at low risk for getting the disease. But as reported in *Time* magazine, women are now contracting AIDS almost as fast as men. It is expected that, by the year 2000, women will make up the majority of people with AIDS worldwide.

Other statistics are just as grim. In the health clinics of San Francisco and New York, two cities in which many people have AIDS, 30 to 50 percent of all new AIDS patients are women. In New York City, AIDS is the leading cause of death among women between the ages of 25 and 34.

There are even cases in which women became infected by having sex with HIV-positive women. At one time, this kind of transmission was thought to be nearly impossible.

Because most of the AIDS research has been on men, doctors sometimes don't recognize the symptoms in women. As a result, women with AIDS are dying at a rate twice as fast as men with AIDS.

A young woman pretends to have died of AIDS at an "Act Up" demonstration in New Orleans.

ROBER
GORDY
KILLED
Reagan/Bush
AIDS Policies

Women with AIDS usually develop some of the same symptoms as infected men. However, they can also develop these complications, which are special to their gender:

- *Recurring vaginal yeast infections*
- *Genital warts*
- *Abnormal vaginal bleeding*
- *Unusually painful menstruation*
- *Genital herpes*

As with all symptoms of AIDS, these could occur in someone without HIV. Only a doctor can determine what these symptoms mean.

People who have unsafe sex or share IV needles with women who have HIV are in danger of contracting the virus, of course. But there are others at risk: the women's children.

About 10,000 children in the United States have HIV today. Most of them probably got the virus from their mothers before they were born. Some of them may have become infected as babies when their mothers breast-fed them.

About a third of all newborn babies of women with HIV are infected with the virus. In these children the infection takes three different patterns.

About a quarter of them develop AIDS symptoms within the first 2 years and die soon afterward. Another group develops less severe symptoms and will live until they are 3 to 5 years old.

The final group has few or no symptoms. Many of these children are not even diagnosed for AIDS until they are 9 or

10 years old. Most die a few years after they develop symptoms. But some are alive today at age 14 and 15.

Growing up with AIDS has its own complications. First of all, many of these children have no mothers. These women have died of AIDS or are too sick to care for their children.

Second, these children usually are troubled by physical problems their whole life. Some of these ailments affect their growth and development.

Finally, they often have severe emotional problems. As they get older, these children begin to realize they are different. They face an uncertain future: How long will they live? How will they deal with being seriously ill? Sometimes the stress is almost too much to bear.

Unlike most infected adults, an HIV-positive child did not get the virus because of risky behavior. Women need to take measures to protect not only themselves, but their future children as well.

African Americans and Latinos

In 1993 the National Commission on AIDS announced that almost half of all people with AIDS in the United States were African American and Latino.

There are many theories as to why the number is so high. One reason is that homosexuality is especially frowned upon in these cultures. As a result, a black or Latino gay man might hide his homosexuality from his friends and family. He might even marry a woman to disguise it. And if he is

HIV-positive, he might not tell anyone because he's afraid of rejection.

Another reason could be that safer sex education has not reached many African Americans and Latinos living in inner cities. People who are poor often do not have easy access to health-care information.

Finally, drug use on the streets of cities has reached an all-time high. The drug culture has taken over entire neighbor-hoods of African Americans and Latinos. This is the main reason AIDS has spread so quickly in these communities.

There are few medical clinics for poor blacks and Hispanics. Those that exist are swamped with clients. They simply can't meet everyone's needs. As a result, the average African American and Latino with AIDS dies sooner than the average white person with AIDS.

Perhaps more than any other group that is at risk, African Americans and Latinos in inner cities have to fight the hard-est to defeat AIDS. The presence of AIDS in these communi-ties is closely tied to both poverty and drugs. And like AIDS, these problems cannot be eliminated overnight. Once again, education about HIV and AIDS may be the only solution to the overwhelming problem.

Teenagers   Many teenagers think they're too young to get AIDS. They're wrong.

Since 1990, the number of AIDS cases among U.S. teenagers has increased about 70 percent. In New York City alone, it is estimated that up to 40,000 teens are infected with HIV. And about 20 percent of all Americans with AIDS became infected when they were teenagers.

Most infected teenagers got HIV from unsafe sex. Most of them knew about AIDS and about practicing safer sex, but, for whatever reason, they chose to ignore the facts.

Some people engage in risky behavior because they are embarrassed to ask their partners to use protection. Others don't feel comfortable talking about safer sex with their partners. And others simply don't think they can get AIDS. A person who doesn't feel comfortable having safer sex shouldn't be having sex at all.

Before teenagers have sex, they must learn to be sexually responsible. That means they should have sex only if they feel ready for it. They have to be able to choose the right partner. And they must take the appropriate steps to avoid unwanted pregnancy and sexually transmitted diseases such as AIDS.

LIVING WITH AIDS

YOU ALREADY KNOW THE PERSON WHO CAN **BEST** PROTECT YOU FROM AIDS.

There is no cure for AIDS. Many people who find out they are HIV-positive or who have AIDS become severely depressed or angry. These are normal reactions for those who face an uncertain future.

These people can also become afraid. They might fear rejection by their loved ones. Or they might be frightened that they'll lose their jobs or homes. And, of course, they are afraid that they will suffer physically and possibly die soon.

Accepting the reality that they have a life-threatening condition will take time. They will need to deal with their fears and their needs. And they will have to learn about the best treatments and the latest research developments.

Fears and Needs

It's not surprising that people with HIV or AIDS fear rejection by their friends and family

Did You Know...?

- About 8 percent of the people with HIV have been infected for up to 14 years and do not have AIDS symptoms.
  Source: ABC News

- The World Health Organization believes that by the year 2000, 30 million people in the world could be infected with HIV. Other researchers believe the number could reach 110 million.
  Source: *Time* magazine, August 3, 1992

- There is 1 AIDS-related death in the United States every 12 minutes.

- Of every 80 babies, 1 is infected with HIV.
  Source: U.S. Advisory Council

members. In fact, most of these people will experience rejection to some extent.

Many people with AIDS notice that some friends or relatives become cool and distant. Perhaps these people are afraid of becoming infected themselves. Or maybe they can't face the reality of the illness. More than likely, they don't know how to handle the disturbing situation, so they stay away.

People with AIDS need all the support they can get. Sharing their feelings with loved ones can help ease their emotional anguish. And if they become physically weak, a friend can relieve some of the sick person's burden.

A person with HIV or AIDS is not alone. Throughout the country, there are support groups for people in the same situation. There are also counselors who treat the emotional needs of infected people. And there are many organizations that can offer medical advice, insurance information, and other kinds of support.

Just as an infected person might feel rejection by a loved one, he or she might feel resentment or hatred from strangers. Many people are afraid of AIDS. Others don't understand it. Frightened and ignorant people often treat people with HIV unfairly. Their attitude is called **discrimination**.

Infected people might experience discrimination in many forms. They might lose their job because their supervisor is afraid of losing clients. Or they might lose their apartment because their landlord thinks that a person can get the virus just by living next door to an infected person. Or their dentist might refuse to treat them because of personal fears.

Perhaps even worse, they might be threatened or physically hurt. There are many instances of abuse against people with AIDS. Insults have been hurled at them, their property has been damaged, and some have even been shot at.

One much-publicized case involved the family of three young boys who were HIV-positive. All three were hemophiliacs who had received contaminated blood products. At first the boys were insulted, threatened, and banned from their elementary school. Eventually their house was burned to the ground, and the family was forced to move from their community.

Most discrimination is against the law. Physical violence is illegal, of course, but so is discrimination by an employer or landlord. Individuals and organizations that provide services cannot discriminate against someone infected with HIV. This means that a doctor or dentist must treat anyone with the virus. And a restaurant cannot refuse to serve a person thought to have AIDS.

All types of discrimination stem from fear and a lack of understanding. Just as education is the best hope for ending AIDS, it is also the best way to end discrimination.

Treatments and Research
Although AIDS has no cure, there are treatments that can prevent illness and prolong life. The first thing people with HIV can do is change their life-style. They need to pay special attention to their diet. They should eat only nutritious foods: fresh fruits

and vegetables, whole grains, and lean meat, such as fish and chicken. They should avoid alcohol, caffeine, and foods that have a lot of fat or sugar.

Giving up smoking and recreational drugs is also necessary. Tobacco and drugs weaken the immune system.

Exercise is an important factor. People who are physically fit have stronger immune systems. Regular exercise will help suppress the virus and may delay AIDS symptoms.

Stress can weaken the immune system, so situations that cause tension should be avoided. Excercise can help relieve stress, and so might acupuncture, yoga, meditation, massage, and prayer.

People with AIDS should also avoid potentially unhealthy activities. These include socializing where there are smokers, visiting people with colds or other viruses, and cleaning up after pets (there are dangerous bacteria in animals' feces and urine).

A few drugs seem to slow the progress of the virus. **AZT**, or azidothymidine, is the most common. It helps prevent the virus from reproducing itself.

But AZT itself has come under attack. Many doctors think that the drug helps at first, but not in the long run. Time magazine recently reported that the drug seems to lose its effectiveness after 18 months. AZT is also highly toxic and can cause side effects in patients.

Some doctors think AZT works best when used with other prescription drugs, such as **ddC**, **ddI**, or **D4T**. These drugs also slow the progress of the virus.

HIV is a complex virus. As it progresses, it can **mutate**. This means the virus can change itself to resist drugs. Researchers believe that taking a combination of treatments makes it more difficult for the virus to build up resistance to medicine.

Doctors are learning more about the effects of AIDS every day. Unfortunately, not all is good news.

About 30 people who have tested negative for HIV are known to have AIDS. Researchers are unsure how this is possible. Some believe that these people have a virus that is related to HIV. Others think that they might have a completely new virus. If this is true, AIDS will become even harder to prevent or cure.

Doctors have also learned how strong HIV really is. First of all, the coating around the virus protects it from almost all drug treatment.

Second, even when a medicine proves to be somewhat effective, the virus changes its chemical makeup to protect itself further. This is why it is taking researchers so long to develop an effective treatment.

Researchers are also unsure when there will be a **vaccine** to protect people from the virus. A vaccine is a type of medicine that will protect a person from a specific virus throughout their life. Vaccines have been developed for diseases such as polio and German measles. But these are caused by more simple viruses than HIV. A vaccine against AIDS will probably not exist until some time in the twenty-first century.

But there is some good news in the world of research. The

AIDS and the Arts

When the actor Rock Hudson died from AIDS-related causes in 1985, many Americans had never heard of the disease. His death alerted the nation to the presence of a life-threatening **epidemic**.

Since then, many more celebrities have died. Their profiles are like those of all people with AIDS. They include men and women, straight and gay, young and old. And they got the virus the same way that other people with AIDS did: from having unprotected gay or straight sex, sharing IV drug needles, or receiving infected blood products.

The death of a celebrity is no more tragic than any other. But when an AIDS-related death makes front-page news, it forces people to think about the crisis and about their own behavior.

Here are some of the most famous names:

Arthur Ashe, professional tennis player

Howard Ashman, lyricist of
The Little Mermaid, Beauty and the Beast, and Aladdin

Michael Bennett, choreographer of A Chorus Line

Amanda Blake, actress on TV's Gunsmoke

Tina Chow, fashion model and designer

Brad Davis, actor who starred in the film Midnight Express

Perry Ellis, fashion designer

Halston, fashion designer

Keith Haring, artist

Liberace, pianist and entertainer

Freddie Mercury, lead singer of the rock group Queen

Rudolf Nureyev, ballet dancer

Anthony Perkins, actor who starred in the film Psycho

Robert Reed, actor on TV's The Brady Bunch

Willi Smith, fashion designer

Ricky Wilson, guitar player for the new-wave band the B-52's

latest is an experimental vaccine for people who are already infected. This vaccine would help the immune system attack the virus. The experiments are still taking place, however. It will be a few years before the vaccine is available for general use.

Other researchers are examining HIV-positive people for common traits. Some of these people have had the virus for 14 years and still do not have AIDS. Doctors are trying to learn if there is something in their physical makeup preventing them from developing full-blown AIDS. If these people have a special trait, perhaps it can be duplicated in others.

Some scientists are exploring gene therapy. They believe that a person's genes can be changed to make the cells inhospitable to HIV—that is, the cells reject the virus. There has been some success in test tubes, but doctors haven't been able to translate their findings to humans yet.

Research on AIDS seems to change every day. It is important that people with HIV or AIDS stay informed about these new developments.

We do not have a cure or a vaccine or even a completely effective treatment for AIDS. Until we do, knowledge about the disease and how to prevent it is our best tool to fight it.

FOR MORE
INFORMATION

The National AIDS Hotline
English: (800) 342-AIDS
Spanish: (800) 344-SIDA
Hearing impaired: TDD—1 (800) 243-7889

Centers for Disease Control and Prevention
AIDS Information Office
(404) 329-2891

National AIDS Information Clearinghouse
(800) 458-5231

National Sexually Transmitted Disease Hotline
(800) 227-8922

American Red Cross
(800) 26-BLOOD

American Social Health Association
260 Sheridan Avenue
Palo Alto, CA 94306
(415) 327-6465

National Gay Alliance of Young Adults
P.O. Box 190426
Dallas, TX 75219-0426

GLOSSARY/ INDEX

ABSTINENCE—*19*   The choice of not being sexually active.

AIDS (AQUIRED IMMUNODEFICIENCY SYNDROME)—*5*   A viral disease that affects the immune system and almost always leads to death.

ANTIBODIES—*23*   Blood particles that are manufactured by the immune system to fight infection.

AZT—*42*   A drug that is used to slow the development of HIV.

CONDOM—*21*   A rubber sheath worn on a penis to prevent pregnancy and protect against sexually transmitted diseases.

DDC , DDI, D4T—*42*   Three drugs that are used to slow the progress of HIV.

DEMENTIA—*13*   A brain disorder that often affects people with AIDS.

DENTAL DAM—*21*   A latex square used on a woman's sex organs during oral sex.

DISCRIMINATION—*40*   The unfair treatment of others, especially minorities.

EPIDEMIC—*44*   An outbreak of a disease that affects large numbers of people and is difficult to control.

GAY—*7*   Homosexual.

GRID (GAY-RELATED IMMUNE DEFICIENCY)—*7*   The original name of AIDS.

HEMOPHILIA—*18*   A disease in which blood does not clot properly.

HETEROSEXUAL—*7*   A person who is sexually attracted to members of the opposite sex.

HIV (HUMAN IMMUNODEFICIENCY VIRUS)—*6*   The virus believed to cause AIDS.

HIV-NEGATIVE—*11*   Describing a person who does not have the AIDS virus.

HIV-POSITIVE—*11*   Describing a person who has the AIDS virus.

HOMOSEXUAL—*7*   A person who is sexually attracted to members of the same sex.

IMMUNE SYSTEM—*9*   The body's internal system that fights infection.

IV NEEDLE—*16*   A needle used to shoot drugs into the bloodstream.

KAPOSI'S SARCOMA (ALSO CALLED KS)—*12*   A skin cancer common to people with AIDS.

MUCOUS MEMBRANES—*16*   Spongy, moist layers of cells that line the vagina, rectum, mouth, area around the eyes, and hole in the penis.

MUTATE—*43*   To undergo a physical or chemical change.

NONOXYNOL-9—*21*   A condom lubricant that helps kill HIV.

PROMISCUITY—*27*   Behavior that is exemplified by having many sex partners.

SAFER SEX—*21*   Sexual activity that prevents body fluids from coming into contact with sex organs and mucous membranes.

STRAIGHT—*7*   Heterosexual.

T CELLS—*9*   Blood cells that are part of the immune system. HIV attacks these cells.

THRUSH—*12*   A type of yeast infection that produces a thick, whitish coating in the mouth and throat.

TRANSFUSION—*18*   The medical process in which a patient receives another person's blood.

TRANSPLANT—*18*   An operation in which a diseased or damaged body organ is replaced with a healthy organ from someone else.

VACCINE—*43*   A drug that will protect a person from a specific viral infection for life.

VIRUS—*6*   A tiny germ that can cause illness in animals and plants.